Legacy Data Evaluation Report for Amistad National Recreation Area

Natural Resource Report NPS/CHDN/NRR-2011/297

James Von Loh

Cogan Technology, Inc.
8140 East Lightening View Drive
Parker, Colorado 80134

Dan Cogan

Cogan Technology, Inc.
21 Valley Road
Galena, Illinois 61036

February 2011

U.S. Department of the Interior
National Park Service
Natural Resource Program Center
Fort Collins, Colorado

The National Park Service, Natural Resource Program Center publishes a range of reports that address natural resource topics of interest and applicability to a broad audience in the National Park Service and others in natural resource management, including scientists, conservation and environmental constituencies, and the public.

The Natural Resource Report Series is used to disseminate high-priority, current natural resource management information with managerial application. The series targets a general, diverse audience, and may contain NPS policy considerations or address sensitive issues of management applicability.

All manuscripts in the series receive the appropriate level of peer review to ensure that the information is scientifically credible, technically accurate, appropriately written for the intended audience, and designed and published in a professional manner.

This report received informal peer review by subject-matter experts who were not directly involved in the collection, analysis, or reporting of the data.

Views, statements, findings, conclusions, recommendations, and data in this report do not necessarily reflect views and policies of the National Park Service, U.S. Department of the Interior. Mention of trade names or commercial products does not constitute endorsement or recommendation for use by the U.S. Government.

This report is available from NPS Chihuahuan Desert Network website (http://science.nature.nps.gov/im/units/chdn/) and the Natural Resource Publications Management website (http://www.nature.nps.gov/publications/NRPM).

Please cite this publication as:

VonLoh, J. and D. Cogan. 2011. Legacy data evaluation report for Amistad National Recreation Area. Natural Resource Report NPS/CHDN/NRR—2011/297. National Park Service, Fort Collins, Colorado.

NPS 621/106602, February 2011

Contents

Figure

Tables

Appendix

Executive Summary

The National Park Service (NPS)-Chihuahuan Desert Network (CHDN) and Amistad National Recreation Area (AMIS and NRA), with the assistance of the National Vegetation Inventory Program (NVIP) staff, is preparing to conduct vegetation classification plot sampling in support of creating a vegetation map, geodatabase, and final report beginning in spring 2011. As part of study plan (NPS-AMIS 2010) preparation, historic or legacy data were identified for evaluation to determine if existing useful data can be used and thus save costs by reducing the amount of new data collection.

Discussions with the CHDN science advisor and data manager, AMIS natural resources staff, and employing Internet searches resulted in identification of 10 potentially useful studies or databases (NPS-AMIS 2010). During study plan preparation, the research studies and datasets were divided by potential use into project background and local vegetation type description utility (seven studies), geo-referenced information with a variety of project utility applications, particularly bio-physical unit (BPU) development under a gradient-oriented transect (gradsect) application (two studies), and studies that would be useful for vegetation classification and to reduce sampling efforts providing project economy (one study). Following initial review, some studies were dropped from consideration and other studies were added as they were located; 11 studies and databases were evaluated in detail herein.

The purpose of Task 1.0: Legacy Data Evaluation for AMIS, is primarily to evaluate existing (legacy) data for usefulness in the vegetation classification at AMIS and secondarily to provide usable legacy data in the project gradsect to reduce time and costs for the labor-intensive field sampling task. Legacy studies and databases generally form two groups, e.g., vegetation classification information or plant species lists. In general, the group of legacy studies for AMIS and vicinity provide excellent plant species lists, descriptions of physical resources (topography, geology, soils, hydrology, etc.), historic landscape photography, and vegetation classification based primarily on observation and frequency determination. Useful data were received and analyzed in this study, the most useful information occurred in the eight studies summarized in Table 1.

The most significant on-park vegetation studies, Poole (2004) and Larson (2002), were summarily evaluated by NVIP Ecologist Chris Lea (2009) and fell within utility Category II. Mr. Lea did not recommend the Poole (2004) dataset to replace classification plot sampling, but he considered the data helpful in terms of sampling efficiency by identifying the more species-diverse (and possibly more community-diverse) sites that could be targeted during planning as the best places to locate several community types for sampling. No savings to the field sampling of classification plot data task, in terms of field crew costs or time to sample reduced numbers of new plots, were determined relative to this legacy data analysis. An unknown cost saving will result from having a more efficiently designed sampling plan and a well-informed gradsect analysis to guide field crews.

Table 1. Summary Analysis of the Most Significant Vegetation Legacy Datasets to Inform the AMIS Vegetation Inventory Project

Research Date Author	Utility Cat.	Description	No. of Plots	Discussion	Recommendations	Sample Status
1901 Bray	III	Five major vegetation formations were observed and described in the early 1900s: (1) Grass [Close, Open Bunch, Salt]; (2) Woody [Xerophytic Forest Formation of the Mountain Slopes of Trans-Pecos Texas and Mesophytic Forest Formations of the Streamways]; (3) Succulent [Agave, Sotol, Yucca, Lechuguilla, Cacti]; (4) Rock [Creosote bush, Mesquite]; and (5) Halophytic [Salt Grass].	0	The information does not describe existing conditions within AMIS; the late 19th century / early 20th century landscape photographs are informative.	Use this early ecological paper to describe the historic condition of portions of AMIS.	N/A
1982 Golden, Gabriel, and Stevens	III	37 soils mapping units were described and prepared into a coverage map for AMIS and the greater Val Verde County area during the 1970s and 1980s. Because of development potential, the soils of AMIS were mapped in greater detail.	0	The information describes existing conditions within AMIS in terms of an important vegetation driver. The mid-to-late 20th century landscape photographs are informative. Lists of dominant plant species aided development of the alliance/association list for the project.	This valuable account of geology, soils, and existing vegetation would be useful to inform the local vegetation alliance and plant association descriptions and appropriate historical and edaphic summary sections of the final report. The soils map will also provide a relevant coverage in the project geodatabase.	N/A
2004 Poole	II	The 706 plant species known for AMIS as a result of this study form 76 vegetation types at the association level determined by the author from species frequency data and observations.	0	The information allowed partial development of a provisional classification list to the association level and provided important information during gradsect development to inform the upcoming vegetation classification and mapping project within AMIS.	This valuable botanical account of AMIS will be useful to inform the historical and existing context of AMIS vegetation and will aid in writing local vegetation alliance and plant association descriptions. The entire plant species list will be useful to botanists sampling field data for this project by informing taxonomic decisions during field work.	Lea evaluated the dataset in 2009

Table 1. Summary Analysis of the Most Significant Vegetation Legacy Datasets to Inform the AMIS Vegetation Inventory Project

Research Date Author	Utility Cat.	Description	No. of Plots	Discussion	Recommendations	Sample Status
2002 Worthington	III	Dr. Worthington examined literature, herbaria records, and conducted site visits, then submitted a working draft of 618 vascular plant species known to occur in AMIS.	0	Dr. Worthington prepared tables with plant species known to occur in AMIS. The tabular data were divided into families and each taxa was described by scientific name and author, common name, and known location within the NRA.	With updates by the focused inventory of Poole (2004), it formed the basis of the plant species list for the study plan (NPS-AMIS 2010), the field data collection manual, the provisional list of vegetation alliances and plant associations, and will be included in the project final report and geodatabase.	N/A
2002 Larson	III	Mr. Larson, in a memorandum to Dr. Bill Reid of CHDN, proposed eight vegetation structures or types and two landforms to represent a majority of the plant communities within AMIS.	0	The 10 vegetation structures proposed by Mr. Larson are: (1) *Prosopis glandulosa* Woodland; (2) *Quercus fusiformis - Celtis laevigata* Woodland; (3) *Acacia minuata (farnesiana)* Woodland; (4) *Acacia minuata (farnesiana)* Shrubland; (5) *Acacia rigidula - Leucophyllum frutescens - Acacia berlandieri* Shrubland; (6) *Prosopis glandulosa* Shrubland; (7) *Phragmites australis* Herbaceous Vegetation; (8) *Hilaria berlangeri – Bouteloua curtipendula* Herbaceous Vegetation; (9) Rock Outcrop / Butte Sparse Vegetation; and (10) Open Cliff Sparse Vegetation.	The information allowed partial development of a provisional classification to the alliance level to support field crews and inform the upcoming vegetation classification and mapping project within AMIS.	Lea evaluated the dataset in 2009

Table 1. Summary Analysis of the Most Significant Vegetation Legacy Datasets to Inform the AMIS Vegetation Inventory Project

Research Date Author	Utility Cat.	Description	No. of Plots	Discussion	Recommendations	Sample Status
2007 Von Loh, Janssen	II	30 mostly riparian plots describing 12 vegetation types / map units in five ecological systems were collected along the Rio Grande approximately 8-10 miles downstream of AMIS.	30 off-park	Off-park surveys of riparian and limited upland plant communities along approximately 4 miles of the Rio Grande near Del Rio, Texas, were conducted to classify, map, and evaluate impacts related to tactical infrastructure installation on the U.S.-Mexico border. Nearly 30 observation points (dominant species structure and cover data, habitat data, site notes, species lists, location information, and digital photographs) were sampled to prepare descriptions to the vegetation alliance and plant association level of the NVC and prepare a vegetation map. Twelve riparian and upland vegetation types were described and delineated using 2007 NAIP imagery for the digital base map product.	The plot data were not collected within AMIS boundaries; however, elements of the classification do occur within AMIS on the Rio Grande floodplain as verified by a December 2009 site visit by one of the authors. The data would be useful to inform descriptions of vegetation alliances/plant associations, examine the quality of 2007 NAIP imagery, develop photo-signatures, and guide interpretation following formal vegetation classification.	Data available from DHS, USBP
1995 Texas Parks & Wildlife Dept. (TPWD), TNHP, RPD	III	At the time of this study, the AMIS NRA site occupied 107 acres under U.S. Air Force management; some of the area was inundated.	0	The plant species list included 59 families and 200 species from inventories conducted in 1993 and 1994; no rare plant species were observed. Four vegetation series were named: (1) Curly Mesquite – Sideoats Grama Series; (2) Cenizo Series; (3) Guajillo Series; and (4) Blackbrush Series. The Blackbrush Series dominated the entire site. Drainages	The data were used by others to develop the current plant species list provided in the study plan, were used to prepare the provisional list of alliances/associations, and would likely be useful to inform the historical context of AMIS vegetation types and possibly to aid in writing local vegetation alliance and plant association descriptions.	N/A

Table 1. Summary Analysis of the Most Significant Vegetation Legacy Datasets to Inform the AMIS Vegetation Inventory Project

Research Date Author	Utility Cat.	Description	No. of Plots	Discussion	Recommendations	Sample Status
				supported linear stands of netleaf hackberry, Texas kidneywood, and Roemer's acacia. The fluctuating reservoir shoreline supported salt-cedar, tree tobacco, and Rooseveltweed.		
1999 Texas Parks & Wildlife Dept. (TPWD)	II	This report primarily discusses the 37 vegetation monitoring plots established in Devils River State Natural Area (DRSNA) between September 1996 and September 1997. DRSNA is approximately 30 miles north of AMIS. Locations were initially plotted on a 7.5-minute topographic map (Dolan Springs Quadrangle) and later, each plot origin point was geo-referenced in GIS format using a Trimble Geoexplorer II Unit and converted into a shapefile for use in ArcView applications. The procedures used in the establishment of monitoring plots generally followed the protocol outlined in the Western Region Fire Monitoring Handbook (NPS 1992); initial data analyses were performed using the corresponding software package, FMH ver. 2.1u (Syoriak 1997). The research is supported by a comprehensive species list containing 489 plant taxa occurring within DRSNA.	37 off-park	Monitoring plots were located within 10 of the 11 series-level communities identified within DRSNA: (1) Curlymesquite-Sideoats Grama Series (12 plots); (2) Mesquite-Whitebrush Series (5 plots); (3) Ceniza Series (4 plots); (4) Ashe Juniper-Oak Series (2 plots); (5) Lechuguilla-Sotol Series (3 plots); (6) Guajillo Series (3 plots); (7) Sycamore-Willow Series (2 plots); (8) Netleaf Hackberry-Little Walnut Series (2 plots); (9) Apache Plume Series (2 plots); (10) Plateau Live Oak-Netleaf Hackberry Series (2 plots); and (11) Maidenhair Fern - Southern Shieldfern Series (not monitored).	The data were used to prepare the provisional list of alliances / associations and would likely be useful to inform the classification, descriptions of vegetation alliances / plant associations, examine the quality of 2007 NAIP imagery, develop photo-signatures, and guide interpretation following formal vegetation classification.	Data available from TPWD

x #

Introduction

CHDN and AMIS, with the assistance of the NVIP staff, are preparing to conduct vegetation classification plot sampling in support of creating a vegetation map, geodatabase, and final report beginning in spring 2011. Funding will be awarded to qualified botanists/ecologists for initial field data collection in the form of classification plots as described in the project study plan (NPS-AMIS 2010). Field crews benefit from having a field sampling plan containing a preliminary list of vegetation alliances and plant associations, developed from appropriate legacy datasets and the park plant species list from which to inform landscape observations of vegetation stands, classification plot site selection, plot density, and provisional plant community type decisions when sampling vegetation types for classification under the NVC.

The legacy data evaluated herein were collected by or submitted to CHDN and AMIS staffs historically and along with interviews with responsible researchers directly involved in legacy data gathering comprise the results of this report. Results generated from this study were also used to prepare the gradsect (Task 2.0: Gradsect and Field Sampling Plan for AMIS and to supplement the list of potential vegetation alliances and plant associations (Task 3.0: Vegetation Classification List Update for AMIS). Please refer to the study plan (NPS-AMIS 2010) for additional information explaining project tasks, examples, timing, and budget estimates.

The NVC, as developed by The Nature Conservancy (TNC) and currently maintained by NatureServe (2010), represents a national system containing seven levels: (1) Formation Class, (2) Formation Subclass, (3) Formation, (4) Division, (5) Macrogroup, (6) Group, (7) Alliance, and (8) Association, with the finest level being the plant association. Alliances are usually aggregations of associations that are physiognomically uniform and share one or more characteristic or diagnostic species. An association is defined as a plant community or type with a consistent species composition, uniform physiognomy, and homogenous habitat conditions (Flahault and Schroter 1910). The plant association or community type is determined by environmental patterns and disturbance processes.

Associations are separated from alliances through the use of total floristic composition and are named by the most dominant and/or indicator species. For the name or title assigned to an association or alliance, a single dominant species may be used (*Prosopis glandulosa* Woodland). If two dominant species of the same stratum are used they are separated by a dash (*Acacia berlandieri – Leucophyllum frutescens* Shrubland). If two dominant species occur in different strata, then a slash is used to separate them (*Prosopis glandulosa / Panicum virgatum* Woodland). Parentheses are used when the diagnostic species are not consistent in the association or alliance (i.e., *Bothriochloa ischaemum – (Pappophorum bicolor)* Herbaceous Vegetation).

The purpose of the NVC is to provide a complete, standardized listing and description of all vegetation types that represent the variation in biological diversity at the community level and to identify those communities that require protection (Grossman et al. 1994). The NVC focuses on existing vegetation rather than potential natural vegetation, climax vegetation, or physical habitats. Because it is not restricted to static vegetation types, classification units are useful both for inventory, site description, and as the basis for building dynamic ecological models. The

NVC also includes vegetation along the natural-invasive-cultural (semi-natural and modified) continuum, but it emphasizes natural communities as the focus of biodiversity protection.

Typical vegetation stands sampled under the NVIP equal or exceed the project minimum mapping unit (MMU) of 0.5 hectare (1.24 acres). Unique vegetation patches less than the MMU may also be sampled using vegetation classification plots or less rigorous observation points. Small patches or stands are often termed "park specials" in the NVIP because of their value for overall management prescriptions. Resource management staff at AMIS identified such stands of unique vegetation at the AMIS Study Plan (NPS-AMIS 2010) kick-off meeting. Typically, between three to five classification plots are required to adequately describe most vegetation alliances and plant associations.

Background

The following discussion was excerpted in part from the AMIS Study Plan (NPS-AMIS 2010) and users are encouraged to review the plan to place this legacy research study in context with the larger project. Uninundated reaches of the Rio Grande and Pecos and Devils rivers support most of the woodland and forest vegetation types. The majority of AMIS vegetation consists of thornscrub shrubland communities and some sparsely vegetated rock outcrops. A broad drawdown zone can occur on the reservoir shoreline that may be unvegetated or may support shrubland or herbaceous vegetation types if the drawdown occurred over several growing seasons.

The TPWD (2009) describes this reach of the Rio Grande under the Trans-Pecos, Edwards Plateau, and South Texas Brush Country (Rio Grande Basin) Natural Regions and the Level III Ecoregions of the South Texas Plains, Edwards Plateau, and Trans-Pecos. During 2007-2008, the DHS-USBP used the NVC to describe the vegetation of the Rio Grande floodplain and adjacent toeslopes and canyons in the Del Rio Sector (DHS-USBP 2008). Poole (2004) recorded plant species frequency on pre-selected sites to prepare a plant species list for AMIS and reported 76 different plant communities. Two major vegetation types are described in the AMIS General Management Plan (2006)—Floodplain/Upland Riparian and Scrub Desert and Thornscrub.

Floodplain/Upland Riparian: consists of seven general categories including Chihuahuan Desert Scrub, Tamaulipan Floodplain, Thornscrub, Savannah, and North American Arid West Emergent Marsh (USBP 2008). The Rio Grande, Devils River, and Pecos River have high water tables and dependable year-round flows and where not confined by steep canyon walls support dense stands of vegetation. Nonnative salt cedar or tamarisk and giant reed or carrizo are being systematically removed from some reaches of the Rio Grande allowing native riparian and wetland plants to reestablish.

Scrub Desert and Thornscrub: this vegetation structure was compiled from 76 plant communities listed in Poole (2004), 10 vegetative structures from Larson (2002), and corresponding types including Chihuahuan Desert Scrub and Tamaulipan Thornscrub vegetation described by USBP (2008). Desert scrub is characterized by shrubs and succulents. Grasses are understory or occur in small patches and typically provide insufficient fuels to carry fire. Scrub Desert occurs on toeslopes, hills, and cliffs adjacent to the river floodplains and above the reservoir high-water line.

Project area vegetation distribution is influenced by several factors (ecologic drivers) that include hydrology, elevation, slope, aspect/slope exposure, precipitation patterns, temperature extremes, topographic position, geology, and soils. The environmental drivers are discussed in detail and used to prepare BPU maps in support of field crews in the companion study (Task 2.0: Gradsect and Field Sampling Plan for AMIS).

The Rio Grande annual flows and sediment delivery/removal have been controlled by Amistad Dam and upstream dams and groundwater pumping for many decades resulting in diminished overbank flooding and allowing bank-armoring vegetation including salt-cedar (*Tamarix* spp.), giant reed (*Arundo donax*), Johnson grass (*Sorghum halepense*), buffelgrass (*Cenchrus ciliaris*), and Bermuda grass (*Cynodon dactylon*) to become established on riverbanks, point bars, and islands. These invasive, nonnative species have become a management concern and the assignment of AMIS resources to monitor populations and attempt focused control and eradication methods has occurred. Nonnative vegetation types that meet the MMU are routinely sampled for classification and mapping purposes under the NVIP.

Legacy Data and Existing Vegetation Maps

Legacy data are existing qualitative and quantitative vegetation information and vegetation maps collected/created prior to recreation area establishment and in support of a variety of AMIS research projects over the decades since designation. Guidance has been prepared to aid the evaluation of existing vegetation datasets (TNC 1996) that is summarized in Appendix 1; the flow chart allows ecologists to place each dataset into a utility category (I-V) representing usefulness of the data for vegetation classification and mapping. The utility categories presented herein use this flow chart and the accompanying descriptions. All legacy studies are potentially useful to this project in various ways, typically to provide historical perspective and contribute to local lant associationdescriptions during final report preparation; the most important studies are presented and discussed below and in Tables 1 and 2. The most important vegetation datasets to inform this project are relatively recent, accurately geo-referenced, have complete species lists, provide estimates of vegetation structure and cover, and describe edaphic elements.

Previous Vegetation Studies at AMIS

As presented in the study plan (NPS-AMIS 2010), 10 legacy vegetation studies were initially acquired from Internet searches, AMIS staff, and/or provided by Hildy Reiser, CHDN science advisor and Missy Powell, CHDN data manager. They were divided into three preliminary groups based on perceived vegetation inventory project utility: (1) General Project Background Information, (2) Potential Category II, or (3) Potential Category I.

Studies and datasets originally placed within the General Project Background Information section (seven studies) are dated and were expected to be useful to support historical context in the final project report (background and history sections, land-use discussion, local vegetation type descriptions, plant species list, etc.) and to support local vegetation alliance and plant association descriptions. This group of documents was further evaluated herein and the following were placed into utility categories II (data are adequate to assist in photo-interpretation, photographic signature key development, or map accuracy assessment) and III (data can be used for vegetation classification and characterization of a vegetation type within the NRA, but not for

3

mapping or analysis because the sample is not adequately geo-referenced, contains inadequate detail in the vegetation information, and/or may not represent existing vegetation at the sample location): Poole and Hedges (1999), Bray (1901); Van Auken et al. (1979), TNHP (1995), and Worthington (2002). Each evaluated dataset and study is described in detail within Table 2 in the results section.

Both datasets and studies originally placed under potential category II in the study plan (NPS-AMIS 2010), the research prepared by Poole (2004) and Larson (2002) was analyzed in detail in Table 2 in the results section. These datasets and reports were placed into utility categories II and III generally due to their lack of classification plot data and reliance on field observation and/or frequency data. The plant species frequency data Poole collected (early 2000s) from sites selected to develop the species list, survey for rare plant species, and prepare a classification list to the alliance/association level were evaluated by Chris Lea, NVIP ecologist, to determine their utility to possibly reduce/replace new data collection and reduce project costs. The vegetation alliance/association list (Poole 2004) and the vegetative structure list (Larson 2002) were incorporated into the project vegetation alliance/plant association list, many as provisional types, to guide field crew members.

The dataset, map, and report originally listed under potential category I in the study plan (NPS-AMIS 2010) was analyzed in detail in Table 2 in the results section. This dataset and report was placed in utility category II (data are adequate to assist in photo-interpretation, photographic signature key development, or map accuracy assessment) because although recent was sampled along the Rio Grande about 8-10 miles off-park.

An additional group of four vegetation studies and plant species lists emerged under this contract task and are examined in further detail and summarized in Table 2 in the results section. These datasets, soils maps, and reports were placed in utility categories II, III, and IV (dataset was assessed and not found to be useful at any level).

Preliminary Vegetation Alliance / Plant Association and Species Lists

Lists of vegetation alliances and plant associations that could occur within AMIS were prepared to support study plan (NPS-AMIS 2010) cost estimates and to inform field crews during the sampling phase. Please refer to the companion study (Task 3.0: Vegetation Classification List Update for AMIS) and the AMIS Study Plan (2010) for an in-depth summary of this project task. Several new vegetation alliances and plant associations, including semi-natural types, were added to this list as a result of legacy data evaluation.

Effect on Field Data Collection Approach

Based on reservoir acreage, AMIS is categorized as a large park (TNC 1994b) for vegetation inventory and mapping; however, in terms of uninundated upland area it is of the moderate size. Large park units are best sampled by first identifying each unique ecoregion and/or management zone and then creating separate modified gradsects (gradient-oriented transects) (Austin and Heyligers 1989) and BPU maps for each ecoregion / management zone in the NRA. The resulting BPUs can then be used to guide field crews, develop cost surfaces, and focus vegetation sampling. This BPU sampling design was based on the premise that if the field crews visit the full spectrum of physical environments at easy to moderately difficult-to-access representative sites, in a step-wise fashion, then most of the vegetation types would be economically sampled. Modifications of these methods have been statistically shown to capture more information than standard designs based on sampling systematic grids (Gillison and Brewer 1985, and Austin and Heyligers 1989).

Cogan Technology, Inc. (CTI) GIS staff cooperated with the CHDN and AMIS GIS staffs to create the BPUs and the overall field sampling design under Task 2.0: Gradsect and Field Sampling Plan for AMIS of this contract. Effective ecoregion/management zones identified by AMIS staff during the project planning meeting included: (1) Rio Grande, Devils River, and Pecos River Riparian, (2) Reservoir (up to ordinary high water), (3) Islands, (4) East of State Highway (SH) 90, and (5) West of SH 90. A map of BPU polygons for AMIS, the UTM coordinates of each polygon centroid, and a field sampling scheme was prepared by CTI with assistance from the legacy data analyzed herein, particularly Poole (2004) and Golden et al. (1982).

To help guide the field collection of vegetation classification data, preliminary BPU polygons were selected as potential sampling sites through a combination of local expertise, access, physical characteristics, and the existing soils map and frequency sampling data. Standard ancillary datasets including soils, geology, and hydrology (including seep and spring locations) for the area could also be used to assist in sample site selection. Potentially useful legacy data have been identified for AMIS and were evaluated for this document by experienced NVIP and contract ecologists.

Results

Several vegetation, soils, and hydrology classifications, datasets, and species lists were evaluated during this project planning task. The datasets and studies were evaluated under the criteria of Appendix 1 and the results were summarized in Table 2; pertinent support information and data tables were copied into Appendix 2.

Bray (1901) determined five major vegetation formations within AMIS that he further discussed as three forested subformations, three grassland formations, and seven shrubland formations. Also interesting within Bray's research are the representatvie black-and-white photograph reproductions that depict the landscape and distribution/cover of vegetation in an era of intense livestock grazing and browsing. Golden, Gabriel, and Stevens (1982) mapped 37 soil associations in AMIS that have been summarized relative to dominant plant communities and diagnostic plant species in Table 2-1, Appendix 2. Due to development concerns around the reservoir, AMIS soils were mapped at a higher level of detail than were soils in the outlying portions of Val Verde County. The soils layer contributed significantly to the gradsect development task of this project, which is described separately.

NatureServe (2003) ecologists prepared global descriptions that were excerpted from a nationwide database prepared in 2002. They included pertinent descriptions of 29 vegetation alliances and 48 plant associations that have already been classified within the NVC and most of which appear on the list of plant communities developed for AMIS. The vegetation classification data and map prepared by DHS-USBP (2008) was managed by contract ecologists Jim Von Loh and Gena Janssen, who used the approach of the NVIP and NatureServe classifications to create the species list and prepare vegetation descriptions and GIS products. These data were keyed within utility category II: "Data are adequate to assist in photo interpretation, photographic signature key development, or map accuracy assessment (i.e., the vegetation and site information are of lower quality, but the samples represent existing vegetation and are geo-referenced with reasonable confidence)." However, these data were recorded off-park in the Rio Grande floodplain on the edge of the city of Del Rio to the east of AMIS. Approximately 30 observation points were recorded that represented five ecological systems and 12 vegetation alliances / plant associations; these types contributed to the potential list of vegetation alliances / plant associations prepared in the study plan (NPS-AMIS 2010) for field crew reference.

The most significant on-park datasets, Poole (2004) and Larson (2002), were summarily evaluated by NVIP Ecologist Chris Lea (2009) and keyed within utility category II. Mr. Lea did not recommend the Poole (2004) dataset to replace new classification plot sampling, but considered the data helpful in terms of sampling efficiency by identifying the more species-diverse (and possibly more community-diverse) sites that could be targeted during planning as the best places to locate several community types for sampling. The Larson (2002) classification into vegetative structures was based on observation and not on field plots.

Monitoring plots placed within the Devils River State Natural Area (DRSNA) by TPWD (1999) numbered 37 and were established in 10 of the 11 series-level communities identified within DRSNA: (1) Curlymesquite-Sideoats Grama Series (12 plots); (2) Mesquite-Whitebrush Series (5 plots); (3) Ceniza Series (4 plots); (4) Ashe Juniper-Oak Series (2 plots); (5) Lechuguilla-

Sotol Series (3 plots); (6) Guajillo Series (3 plots); (7) Sycamore-Willow Series (2 plots); (8) Netleaf Hackberry-Little Walnut Series (2 plots); (9) Apache Plume Series (2 plots); (10) Plateau Live Oak-Netleaf Hackberry Series (2 plots); and (11) Maidenhair Fern - Southern Shieldfern Series (not monitored). These high-quality data were keyed into utility category II because the sample sites occur off-park approximately 30 miles north of AMIS.

Table 2. Summary of Databases Deemed to be Potentially Useful for the Vegetation Inventory Project of AMIS

Research Title and Date	Utility Category	Discussion	Recommendations
Bray, W. L. 1901. The ecological relations of the vegetation of western Texas. Bot. Gaz. 32(2): 99-123.	III: because the information does not describe existing conditions within western AMIS.	This general discussion of the ecology of the Big Bend region (Trans-Pecos Physiographic Province) was prepared from observations in 1900 and 1901, and contains over 30 black-and-white photographs with lists of dominant species of five major vegetation formations encountered: (1) Grass Formations, (2) Woody Formations, (3) Succulent Formations, (4) Rock Formations, and (5) Halophytic Formations. Bray defined forest and woodland stands under the Xerophytic Forest Formation of the Mountain Slopes of Trans-Pecos Texas and described stands of pinyon pine, juniper, and oak as open and stunted on canyon slopes to closed on alluvial deposits. Forests of the Rio Grande were described under the Mesophytic Forest Formations of the Streamways and included stands of pecan (*Carya illinoensis*), hackberry, elm (*Ulmus pumila*), oak, Texas green ash (*Fraxinus berlandieriana*), and sycamore (*Platanus* spp.) trees. Plains cottonwood (*Populus deltoides*) groves occurred around springs. Shrubland formations described and illustrated with photographs were depicted as mostly open in terms of canopy cover. The most common formations noted were dominated by creosote bush (*Larrea tridentata*), mesquite (*Prosopis glandulosa*), yucca (*Yucca* spp.), sotol (*Dasylirion* spp.), agave (*Agave* spp.), lechuguilla (*Agave lechuguilla*), or species of cacti.

Grasslands of alluvial fans, flats, basins, and playas were described under three formations: (1) Close Grass Formation (grama grasses and other bunchgrasses with dense cover), (2) Open Bunch Grass Formation (grama grasses and other bunchgrasses in open stands on drier sand and gravel deposits), and (3) Salt Grass Formation (saltgrass [*Distichlis spicata*] and other halophiles of alkaline basin bottoms). The annual flora, which were well represented in 1900-1901, was considered part of the grassland formations but also described as "a vegetation phenomenon which periodically overshadows everything else." Bray was impressed with the huge floristic display of bluebonnets (*Lupinus havardii*) and other annual forbs and described their forage value to livestock (cattle, sheep, and goats). One of Bray's conclusions was that profound changes to native vegetation was occurring as a result of disturbed equilibrium (advancement of civilization) and that some species, particularly grasses, were being exterminated; he alluded to establishment of woody or weedy plant species and denudation of hill slopes. | This valuable historical account and photographs occurred during an intense period of livestock grazing and would be useful to inform the historical context of AMIS vegetation in the final report and possibly to aid in writing local vegetation alliance and plant association descriptions. |

Table 2. Summary of Databases Deemed to be Potentially Useful for the Vegetation Inventory Project of AMIS

Research Title and Date	Utility Category	Discussion	Recommendations
Golden, M. L., W. J. Gabriel, and J. W. Stevens. 1982. Soil Survey of Val Verde County, Texas. U. S. Department of Agriculture, Soil Conservation Service in cooperation with the Texas Agricultural Experiment Station and Val Verde County Commissioner's Court. Austin, TX.	III: because the information descrbes existing conditions within AMIS in terms of an important vegetation driver.	This 1982 soil survey includes the entire county; however, the area of AMIS and Del Rio (approximately 400,000 acres) was mapped in narrowly defined units to support future planning and development activities near Lake Amistad. Each of 37 soil mapping units (40 countywide) is supported by soils data and lists of the dominant plant species among other data (**appendix 2; table 2-1**) and the map was used as a vegetation driver to divide physiognomic map units, e.g., woodland, shrubland, herbaceous vegetation, and sparse vegetation from one another during gradsect development under Task 2.0. The soils map was very useful as an element to prepare the gradsect layer and resultant BPUs to guide field research.	This valuable account of geology, soils, existing vegetation, and land use would be useful to inform the local vegetation alliance and plant association descriptions and appropriate historical and edaphic summary sections of the final report. The soils map will also provide a layer in the project geodatabase.
NatureServe 2003. International Classification of Ecological Communities: Terrestrial Vegetation; Tamaulipan Thornscrub Ecoregion. Natural Heritage Central Database. Arlington, VA and San Antonio, TX.	III: because the information is current and provided a basis for partial development of a provisional classification to inform the upcoming vegetation classification and mapping project within AMIS.	These global descriptions developed by NatureServe ecologists were excerpted from a nationwide database prepared in 2002. They included pertinent descriptions of 29 vegetation alliances and 48 plant associations that have already been classified within the NVC. The described plant communities occur along the Rio Grande and other major drainages, their floodplains, and adjacent uplands. Four vegetation alliances, each with one plant association, are dominated by nonnative plant species (salt-cedar, giant reed, common reed, and buffelgrass).	This valuable set of global descriptions will provide a template and basis for describing newly classified alliances and associations at the local level. The appropriate alliance and association names based on the AMIS plant species list was entered into the potential classification list of Task 3.0 will be useful to botanists sampling field data for this project by informing taxonomic decisions during field work.
Texas Parks and Wildlife Department, Texas Natural Heritage Program, Resource Protection Division. 1995. Biological Survey of Lake Amistad Recreation Site, Final Report. For the U.S. Air Force. Austin, TX.	III: because the data are based on ocular reconnaissance and are old, but do describe plant communites currently extant within AMIS.	At the time of this study, the recreation site occupied 107 acres, some inundated. The plant species list included 59 families and 200 species from inventories conducted in 1993 and 1994; no rare plant species were observed. Four vegetation series were named, they are (1) Curly Mesquite – Sideoats Grama Series, (2) Cenizo Series, (3) Guajillo Series, and (4) Blackbrush Series. The Blackbrush Series dominated the entire site. Drainages supported linear stands of netleaf hackberry, Texas kidneywood, and Roemer's acacia. The fluctuating reservoir shoreline supported salt-cedar, tree tobacco, and Rooseveltweed.	The data would likely be useful to inform the historical context of AMIS vegetation and possibly to aid in writing local vegetation alliance and plant association descriptions.

Table 2. Summary of Databases Deemed to be Potentially Useful for the Vegetation Inventory Project of AMIS

Research Title and Date	Utility Category	Discussion	Recommendations
Texas Parks and Wildlife Department, Texas Natural Heritage Program, Resource Protection Division. 1999. Devils River State Natural Area – Baseline Vegetation Study. L. K. Hodges and J. M. Poole. Austin, TX.	II: because the data are not within AMIS boundaries (approximately 30 miles north), the transects are geo-located, the data represent existing vegetation and are adequate for classification and mapping, and the data contain sufficient structural, compositional, and site information and photographs to be placed within the standard classification framework.	As part of the ongoing effort to complete inventories of the natural resources of Devils River State Natural Area (DRSNA), this study was conducted to establish permanent vegetation monitoring plots; the data collected in this exercise will serve as a quantitative baseline inventory for the site. Good information is provided for the site overview, topography, geology, hydrology, soils, and prior studies summaries. DRSNA occurs within the southwestern portion of the Edwards Plateau Vegetational Area (Hatch et al. 1990) and at the junction of three major biological provinces: Balconian, Tamaulipan, and Chihuahuan (Blair 1950) and the natural plant communities exhibit elements of the mesquite-chaparral shrubland of the South Texas Plains, the oak-cedar woodland of the central Edwards Plateau to the east, and the sotol-lechuguilla shrubland of the Trans-Pecos to the west (Smith and Butterwick 1975). To provide improved forage for livestock, large areas of DRSNA were mechanically manipulated through bulldozing, root-plowing, chaining, and hand-clearing, followed by reseeding with nonnative grasses including King Ranch bluestem (*Bothriochloa ischaemum* var. *songarica*), buffelgrass (*Cenchrus ciliaris*), and blue panicgrass (*Panicum antidotale*).

This report primarily discusses the 37 vegetation monitoring plots established in DRSNA between September10, 1996 and September 25, 1997. Locations were initially plotted on a 7.5-minute topographic map (Dolan Springs Quadrangle) and later each plot origin point was geo-referenced in GIS format using a Trimble Geoexplorer II Unit and converted into a shapefile for use in ArcView applications. The procedures used in the establishment of monitoring plots generally followed the protocol outlined in the *Western Region Fire Monitoring Handbook* (NPS 1992); initial data analyses were performed using the corresponding software package, FMH ver. 2.1u (Syoriak 1997). The research is supported by a comprehensive species list containing 489 plant taxa occurring within DRSNA.

Monitoring plots were located within 10 of the 11 series-level communities identified within DRSNA: (1) Curlymesquite-Sideoats Grama Series (12 plots), (2) Mesquite-Whitebrush Series (5 plots), (3) Ceniza Series (4 plots), (4) Ashe Juniper-Oak Series (2 plots), (5) Lechuguilla-Sotol Series (3 plots), (6) Guajillo Series (3 plots), (7) Sycamore-Willow Series (2 plots), (8) Netleaf Hackberry-Little Walnut Series (2 plots), (9) Apache Plume Series (2 plots), (10) Plateau Live Oak-Netleaf Hackberry Series (2 plots), and (11) Maidenhair Fern - Southern Shieldfern Series (not monitored). More plots were established on the grassland mesa tops because prescribed burning was planned to occur on those sites. Each series is described in more detail relative to distr bution and species composition in this report. | The data would be useful to inform the classification, descriptions of vegetation alliances/plant associations, examine the quality of 2007 NAIP imagery, develop photo-signatures, and guide interpretation following formal vegetation classification. |

Table 2. Summary of Databases Deemed to be Potentially Useful for the Vegetation Inventory Project of AMIS

Research Title and Date	Utility Category	Discussion	Recommendations
		Each of the 37 monitoring plots are summarized and tabular data presented from the initial data gathering in the mid-1990s. Included information are: (1) plot identification, (2) establishment date, (3) geo-location, (4) elevation, (5) directions to plot, (6) landform description, (7) list of dominant species from line transects (% frequency, % cover), (8) % native species in plot, (9) average number of species per point, (10) average height, (11) age classes for trees and shrubs (species, age, number, % frequency), and (12) summary of overstory/pole-sized/seedling tree classes (class, species, number, % frequency, basal area, dbh).	
Van Auken, O. W., A. L. Ford, and A. Stein. 1979. A comparison of some woody upland and riparian plant communities of the Southern Edwards Plateau. The Southwestern Naturalist, Vol. 24, No. 1. Pp. 165-180.	III: because the data were not collected within AMIS boundaries, they represent regional ecoregion data; the riparian data represent small creeks that have limited useful data for AMIS drainages, but not the large Rio Grande floodplain upstream and downstream of the reservoir.	This 1978-1979 study focused on the Buda Formation and alluvial deposits (small creeks) of the Edwards Plateau on the edges of the Tamaulipan Thornscrub and the Trans-Pecos Regions. Fourteen sites with relatively mature and undisturbed woodland vegetation were selected to be sampled using the point-centered quarter method to determine major plant community relationships. Although present, shrublands, grasslands, other herbaceous communities, and large creeks or rivers were not sampled. In total, 35 woody species were encountered; 37% were common, 14% occurred only on uplands, and 49% occurred only in riparian habitats. Common trees of the Buda Formation were Mexican juniper (*Juniperus* sp.), live oak (*Quercus* spp.), and Texas persimmon (*Diospyros texanum*); common trees of creeks were Mexican juniper, cedar elm (*Ulmus crassifolia*), sycamore (*Platanus* spp.), and Texas persimmon.	These descriptions and dataset may potentially be used to inform the historic or regional context and local vegetation type descriptions within the final report preparation task.
Von Loh, J. and G. Janssen. 2007. In USDHS; USCBP; USBP. 2008. Environmental Assessment for the proposed construction, operation, and maintenance of tactical infrastructure, USBP Del Rio Sector, TX.	II: because the plot data were not collected within AMIS boundaries (approximately 8-10 miles south); however, elements of the classification do occur within AMIS on the Rio Grande floodplain as verified by a December 2009 site visit by the study plan (NPS-AMIS 2010) authors.	Off-park surveys of plant communities along approximately 4 miles of the Rio Grande adjacent to Del Rio were conducted to classify, map, and evaluate impacts related to proposed tactical infrastructure installation on the U.S.-Mexico border. During November 2007, Mr. Von Loh and Ms. Janssen collected nearly 30 observation points (dominant species structure and cover data, habitat data, site notes, species lists, location information, and digital photographs) to prepare descriptions to the vegetation alliance and plant association level of the NVC and prepare a vegetation map (DHS-USBP 2008). Twelve riparian and upland vegetation types were described and delineated using 2007 NAIP imagery for the digital base map product. Dominant plant species / plant communities encountered in these largely disturbed riparian and floodplain sites included: sugarberry riparian woodland, black willow (*Salix nigra*) woodland, honey mesquite (*Prosopis glandulosa*) woodland and shrubland, granjeno (*Celtis pallida*) woodland and shrubland, huisache (*Acacia farnesiana*) woodland, retama (*Parkinsonia aculeata*) shrubland, Bermuda grass (*Cynodon dactylon*) herbaceous vegetation, giant reed (*Arundo donax*) herbaceous vegetation, narrowleaf cattail (*Typha angustifolia*) emergent wetland, and Russian-thistle (*Salsola kali*) semi-natural herbaceous vegetation. They represented five ecological systems and 12 named or provisional vegetation alliances under the NVC.	The data would be useful to inform descriptions of vegetation alliances / plant associations, examine the quality of 2007 NAIP imagery, develop photo-signatures, and guide interpretation following formal vegetation classification.

Table 2. Summary of Databases Deemed to be Potentially Useful for the Vegetation Inventory Project of AMIS

Research Title and Date	Utility Category	Discussion	Recommendations
Poole, J. M. 2004. An Inventory of the Vascular Plants at Amistad National Recreation Area. Wildlife Diversity Program, Texas Parks and Wildlife Department. Austin, TX.	II: because current data are available; however, the data do not contain sufficient structural, compositional, and site information to be placed within the standard classification framework. Mr. Lea did not recommend this dataset to replace new classification plot sampling, but rather the data might be helpful in terms of sampling efficiency by identifying the more species-diverse (and possibly more community-diverse) sites that could be targeted during planning as the best places to locate several community types for sampling.	Dr. Poole conducted a floristic inventory of AMIS and observed 582 plant species; adding 124 additional species documented within AMIS resulted in a total flora of 706 plant species. She noted that AMIS flora is quite diverse, even with major human-induced disturbances to which the AMIS flora has been subjected (i.e., dam construction, flooding, fluctuating water levels, overgrazing and browsing by abnormally large populations of goats and feral nonnative game species).

Dr. Poole determined 76 plant associations during this research and recommended additional research to determine vegetation classification to the alliance and association levels; the draft plant community list provided with this report represented her educated guess based on single (usually) observations of a site. She stated that her plant community list will be much refined with more intensive work; therefore, it was included in the potential plant community presence list provided to guide field crews during 2011 classification plot sampling as Task 3.0 of this project and considered when preparing the gradsect and BPUs of Task 2.0 of this project.

At each site, Dr. Poole performed a quick visual estimate of species frequency, recording data for each species observed during site visits. As sites were sometimes visited multiple times and often separate lists were made for vegetatively disparate parts of the site (for example uplands vs. inundation zones), a list was developed, combining the frequencies of the same species within the same overall site. The more common frequency was selected for the site, if the temporal or ecological frequencies did not match.

Additionally, Dr. Poole determined an overall frequency level for each plant species for AMIS (the entire recreation area). The two levels of frequency include the "AMIS level" (the entire recreation area), which indicates the poss bility that a given species will be observed at any site and the "site level" (for the individual site within AMIS) suggests how widespread the species is at any given site. Also, some species may primarily or only occur in one part of the site, such as the upland area or the inundation zone; they are referred to as "locally" or "very locally" common, frequent, or abundant at a site. Additionally, a plant may be common to abundant at an individual site, but occur at few sites (i.e., rare at the AMIS level). These plants are labeled "very locally" common or frequent at the AMIS level. On the other hand, a plant may occur at many sites but occur at only a rare or infrequent level at the individual sites; they are represented by a parenthetical modifiers following the main frequency category.

Chris Lea, NVIP ecologist, evaluated Dr. Poole's methods and classification list for utility and poss bly to replace new vegetation plot sampling, as follows: | As presented, the information was used to prepare the plant species list, list of potential plant communities within AMIS, field sampling plan and gradsect, historical context, current vegetation impact types, and may contribute to local vegetation alliance / plant association descriptions. Chris Lea, NVIP ecologist, evaluated the dataset in detail for utility. |

Table 2. Summary of Databases Deemed to be Potentially Useful for the Vegetation Inventory Project of AMIS

Research Title and Date	Utility Category	Discussion	Recommendations
		"I do not think these data would replace plot sampling, but they might be helpful to increase the efficiency of sampling some by identifying more species diverse (and thus, more community diverse) sites that could be targeted as the best places to obtain a number of community types during the visit for sampling. Thus, one might prepare a site (as opposed to plot) classification, by converting the categorical scale of abundance into a numerical ordinal rank using cluster analysis to validate patterns suggested by Poole (where sites correspond to stands or communities) and then target those areas to obtain representative sampling and reduce redundancy in sampling. Sites that were moderate to strong outliers should probably be visited for sampling (with the understanding that there it is more likely that floristically different communities will occur in floristically different sites. But one still needs to visit the site (and entitate the site into communities for sampling, as appropriate) to ascertain whether different communities occur or the sites are simply more diverse or rich versions of other communities.

A site should not be treated as a plot in quantitative analysis (even if the site is homogeneous to community type) because it may represent a much larger (possibly more species rich) area than a plot. In some cases, it may provide supplemental information, if it can be concluded (from comparison with plot data) that the flora list at a site is all from one community type (I suspect it often may be more a mosaic of types). So, my best answer is that site data could be modestly helpful in locating sample sites and may supplement some qualitative descriptions.

The plant community types Poole (and Larson, 2002) observed should be used as initial hypothetical models; 76 is likely too many to consider, but if one placed at least one plot in each of Poole's types, at least most of the variation would be covered, regardless of later splitting or lumping. I tend to split types to guide the sampling (more conservative in catching the full range of variation) then rely on the analysis to explain how much of the splitting employed was real and how much was unrealistic (needs to be lumped—but even then, this approach better ensures that lumped units better span the range of variation).

Dr. Poole mentioned that types were drawn that may imply a map was created. Old vegetation maps (even if not all that accurate) tend to be a better basis for stratifying for sampling than the best gradsect design because they approach a researcher's interpretation of floristic variation, as opposed to a hypothesized environment/flora relationship.

Dr. Poole also described areas of botanical interest within AMIS, they included: (1) the Devils River from Indian Cliffs Canyon upstream (supports many species, | |

Table 2. Summary of Databases Deemed to be Potentially Useful for the Vegetation Inventory Project of AMIS

Research Title and Date	Utility Category	Discussion	Recommendations
		unique here or rarely observed in other areas of AMIS); (2) Satan Canyon (supports wetland and upland canyon areas that are quite floristically unique); (3) the Plateau live oak grove areas including stands in Satan Canyon, Lowry Springs, Live Oak Creek, Seminole Canyon, and Oak Mott in Hunt Area 4 (represent plant communities at the edge of their range); (4) the Graves oak-Texas pistachio community in Pink Cave Cove (and other sites that were not observed during this study are very rare within the United States); (5) the upper portion of the Pecos River above the lake influence (deserves to be restored (i.e., removal of nonnative species) as this area is quite unique as is the upland and cliff face area of the Pecos River picnic and boat launch area); and (6) AMIS land below the dam (although somewhat disturbed, both naturally and by humans, contains many interesting wetlands that may harbor rare plant species). She recommended monitoring and restoration, typically nonnative plant species removal and livestock exclusion, at most sites. The AMIS flora includes 49 nonnative species that represent 7% of the total flora.	
Worthington, R. 2002. Inventory of the flora of Amistad National Recreation Area, Val Verde County, Texas. First Working Draft. Floristic Inventories of the Southwest Program. El Paso, TX.	III: because the information allowed partial development of a provisional classification to inform the upcoming vegetation inventory and mapping project within AMIS.	Dr. Worthington submitted a working draft of plant species known to occur in AMIS. The tabular data were divided into families and each taxa was described by scientific name and author, common name, and known location within the park units. Listed were 618 species of vascular plants (including club mosses and ferns and fern allies).	With updates by the focused inventory of the TPWD-TNHP (2004), it formed the basis of the plant species list for the study plan (NPS-AMIS 2010), the field data collection manual, the provisional list of vegetation alliances and plant associations, and will be included in the project final report and geodatabase.

Table 2. Summary of Databases Deemed to be Potentially Useful for the Vegetation Inventory Project of AMIS

Research Title and Date	Utility Category	Discussion	Recommendations
Larson, D. 2002. Preliminary identification of vegetative structure of Amistad National Recreation Area. Personal Communication to Dr. Bill Reid, Chihuahuan Desert Network Coordinator.	III: because the structural identifications are based on observation and not on sampled data.	Mr. Larson, in a memorandum to Dr. Bill Reid, proposed eight vegetation structures or types and two landforms to represent a majority of plant communities within AMIS, they are: (1) *Prosopis glandulosa* Woodland, (2) *Quercus fusiformis - Celtis laevigata* Woodland, (3) *Acacia minuata (farnesiana)* Woodland, (4) *Acacia minuata (farnesiana)* Shrubland, (5) *Acacia rigidula - Leucophyllum frutescens - Acacia berlandieri* Shrubland, (6) *Prosopis glandulosa* Shrubland, (7) *Phragmites australis* Herbaceous Vegetation, (8) *Hilaria berlangeri – Bouteloua curtipendula* Herbaceous Vegetation, (9) Rock Outcrop / Butte Sparse Vegetation, and (10) Open Cliff Sparse Vegetation. Note: Dr. Poole (2004) did not locate or sample any stands of the *Hilaria berlangeri – Bouteloua curtipendula* Herbaceous Vegetation type as described by Mr. Larson.	These data are useful to prepare the list of plant communities that may be encountered within AMIS, an aid for field crews.
Bowman, I., PhD. 1911. Vegetation of the Texas Region, 1911. Forest Physiography. John Wiley and Sons. New York, NY.	IV: because the data are general and are not current.	Dr. Bowman created a general vegetation map that provides ten regions statewide: (1) Atlantic Forest Belt; (2) Rocky Mountain Forest; (3) Chaparral; (4) Black Prairie; (5) Bolson Desert Flora; (6) Grand Prairie; (7) Great Plains; (8) Transitional with Plains, Prairie, and Atlantic Flora; (9) Coast Prairies; and (10) Yucca Belts. AMIS is within the Bolson Desert Flora and Yucca Belts classifications. The projection is unknown.	The map may be used to place the project in context for a regional floristic discussion in the final project report.

16#

Literature Cited

Austin, M.P. and P.C. Heyligers. 1989. Vegetation survey design for conservation: gradsect sampling of forests in northeastern New South Wales, Biological Conservation. 50:13-32.

Blair, F. W. 1950. The biotic provinces of Texas. *Texas Journal of Science.* 2:1.

Bowman, I., PhD. 1911. Vegetation of the Texas Region, 1911. Forest Physiography. John Wiley and Sons. New York, NY.

Dering, J. Phil. 2002. Amistad National Recreation Area: Archaeological Survey and Cultural Resources Inventory. Del Rio, TX.

Foody, G.M. 1994. On the Compensation for Chance Agreement in Image Classification Accuracy Assessment. Photogrammetric Engineering and Remote Sensing. 58 (10): 1459-1460.

Gauch, H.G. 1982. *Multivariate Analysis in Community Ecology.* Cambridge University Press. New York, NY.

Gillison, A.N. and K.R.W. Brewer. 1985. The use of gradient directed transects of gradsects in natural resource survey. *Journal of Environmental Management.* 20:103-127

Golden, M. L., W. J. Gabriel, and J. W. Stevens. 1982. Soil Survey of Val Verde County, Texas. U. S. Department of Agriculture, Soil Conservation Service in cooperation with the Texas Agricultural Experiment Station and Val Verde County Commissioner's Court. Austin, TX.

Grossman, D.H., D. Faber-Langendoen, A.S. Weakley, M. Anderson, P. Bourgeron, R. Crawford, K. Goodin, S. Landaal, K. Metzler, K. Patterson, M. Pyne, M. Reid, and L. Sneddon. 1998. International classification of ecological communities: Terrestrial Vegetation of the United States. Volume I. The National Vegetation Classification System: development, status, and applications. The Nature Conservancy. Arlington, VA.

Hatch, S. L., K. N. Gandhi, and L. E. Brown. 1990. Checklist of the vascular plant of Texas. The Texas Agriculture Experiment Station, College Station.

Larkin, T.J. and G.W. Bomar. 1983. Climatic Atlas of Texas. Texas Department of Water Resources. Austin, TX.

Larson, D. 2002. Preliminary identification of vegetative structure of Amistad National Recreation Area. Personal Communication to Dr. Bill Reid, Chihuahuan Desert Network Coordinator.

Lea, Chris. 2009. Preliminary evaluation of the TPWD-Poole (2004) dataset in reference to classification plot replacement. NPS-USGS National Vegetation Inventory Project Vegetation Ecologist. Denver, CO.

McCune, B. and M.J. Mefford. 1999. PC-ORD. Multivariate analysis of ecological data, Version 4. MjM Software Design. Gleneden Beach, OR.

National Biological Information Infrastructure. 2007. USGS - NPS Vegetation Mapping Program. Retrieved October 2007 online at: http://www.nbii.gov/about/pubs/factsheet/factsheet4.html.

National Park Service. 2009a. The Chihuahuan Desert Network. Accessed online at: http://science.nature.nps.gov/im/units/chdn/Parks.cfm.

_____. 2009b. Amistad National Recreation Area. Accessed online at: http://www.nps.gov/amis.

_____. 2009c. 12-Step Guidance for NPS Vegetation Inventories. Available online at: http://science.nature.nps.gov/im/inventory/veg/docs/Veg_Inv_12step_Guidance_v1.0.pdf

_____. 2009d. Summary of the Amistad National Recreation Area (AMIS) December 9-10, 2009 Study Plan Meeting. Del Rio, TX.

_____. 2006. Draft General Management Plan / Environmental Assessment. Amistad National Recreation Area, Val Verde County, Texas. Denver, CO.

_____. 2000. Amistad National Recreation Area, Texas; Land Protection Plan. Del Rio, TX.

_____.1992. *Western Region Fire Monitor Handbook*. United States Department of the Interior, San Francisco, CA.

NatureServe 2003. International Classification of Ecological Communities: Terrestrial Vegetation; Tamaulipan Thornscrub Ecoregion. Natural Heritage Central Database. Arlington, VA and San Antonio, TX.

NatureServe Explorer. 2009. An Online Encyclopedia of Life. Accessed online at: www.natureserve.org/explorer.

Poole, J.M. 2004. An Inventory of the Vascular Plants at Amistad National Recreation Area. Wildlife Diversity Program, Texas Parks and Wildlife Department. Austin, TX.

Poole, J.M. and L.K. Hedges. 1999. Devils River State Natural Area – baseline vegetation study. Texas Parks and Wildlife Department. Austin, TX.

Poole, J. M. 2004. An Inventory of the Vascular Plants at Amistad National Recreation Area. Wildlife Diversity Program, Texas Parks and Wildlife Department. Austin, TX.

Smith, J., and M. Butterwick. 1975. A vegetational survey of the Devils River – Dolan Creek area. Pp. 37-57 *in* Devils River: A Natural Area Survey, Park VI of VIII. Division of Natural Resources and Environment, The University of Texas at Austin.

Story, M. 2009. Evaluation of Aerial Imagery on the Southern U.S. Border. NPS – Natural Resources Program Center. Office of Inventory, Monitoring, and Evaluation. Denver, CO.

Syoriak, W. A. 1996. NPS Fire Monitoring Handbook software version 2.1u.

Texas Natural Heritage Program. 1995. Biological Survey of Lake Amistad Recreation Site. Final Report. Texas Parks and Wildlife Department, Austin, TX.

Texas Parks and Wildlife Department, Texas Natural Heritage Program, Resource Protection Division. 1995. Biological Survey of Lake Amistad Recreation Site, Final Report. For the U.S. Air Force. Austin, TX.

Texas Parks and Wildlife Department, Texas Natural Heritage Program, Resource Protection Division. 1999. Devils River State Natural Area – Baseline Vegetation Study. L. K. Hodges and J. M. Poole. Austin, TX.

The Nature Conservancy (TNC). 1996. Final Draft Methodology for Assessing the Utility of Existing Data for Vegetation Mapping. NBS/NPS Vegetation Mapping Program. Prepared for the United States Department of Interior, Biological Resources Division and National Park Service. December 1996.

The Nature Conservancy and Environmental Systems Research Institute. 1994a. NBS/NPS Vegetation Mapping Program: Final Draft, Standardized National Vegetation Classification System. Prepared for USDI – National Biological Survey and National Park Service. Arlington, VA.

The Nature Conservancy (TNC) and Environmental Systems Research Institute (ESRI). 1994. Final Draft Accuracy Assessment Procedures. NBS/NPS Vegetation Mapping Program. Prepared for the United States Department of Interior, Biological Resources Division and National Park Service. November 1994.

The Nature Conservancy and Environmental Systems Research Institute. 1994b. NBS/NPS Vegetation Mapping Program: Final Draft, Field Methods for Vegetation Mapping. Prepared for USDI – National Biological Survey and National Park Service. Arlington, VA.

U.S. Department of Agriculture, Natural Resources Conservation Service (USDA, NRCS). 2001. PLANTS Database. Retrieved November 2001, from (http://plants.usda.gov/home_page.html).

——— Soil Conservation Service. 1982. Soil Survey, Val Verde County, Texas. In cooperation with: Texas Agricultural Experiment Station and Val Verde County Commissioners Court. Austin, TX.

U.S. Department of Homeland Security (DHS). 2008. Environmental Assessment for the Proposed Construction, Operation, and Maintenance of Tactical Infrastructure. U.S. Border Patrol. Del Rio Sector, TX.

U.S. Geological Survey (USGS). 1985. Amistad National Recreation Area, Del Rio and Vicinity; Texas-Coahuila, 1:50,000-scale metric topographic map. Denver, CO.

Van Auken, O. W., A. L. Ford, and A. Stein. 1979. A comparison of some woody upland and riparian plant communities of the Southern Edwards Plateau. The Southwestern Naturalist, Vol. 24, No. 1. Pp. 165-180.

Von Loh, J. and G. Jannsen. 2007. In USDHS; USCBP; USBP. 2008. Environmental Assessment for the proposed construction, operation, and maintenance of tactical infrastructure, USBP Del Rio Sector, TX.

Worthington, R. D. 2002. Preliminary inventory of the flora of Amistad National Recreation Area and surrounding area, south-central Val Verde County, Texas; second working draft. Floristic Inventories of the Southwest Program, El Paso, TX.

Worthington, R. 2002. Inventory of the Flora of Amistad National Recreation Area, Val Verde County, Texas. First Working Draft. Floristic Inventories of the Southwest Program. El Paso, TX.

Appendix 1: Evaluating Existing Datasets

Figure 1-1 presents a step-by-step process to evaluate existing datasets according to seven components for their utility in vegetation mapping. Starting from the top of the figure, datasets are assessed and placed into appropriate categories of utility.

Each step of the process, as it is linked to the seven factors, is further described below.

Figure 1-1. Flow Chart for Evaluating Existing Datasets

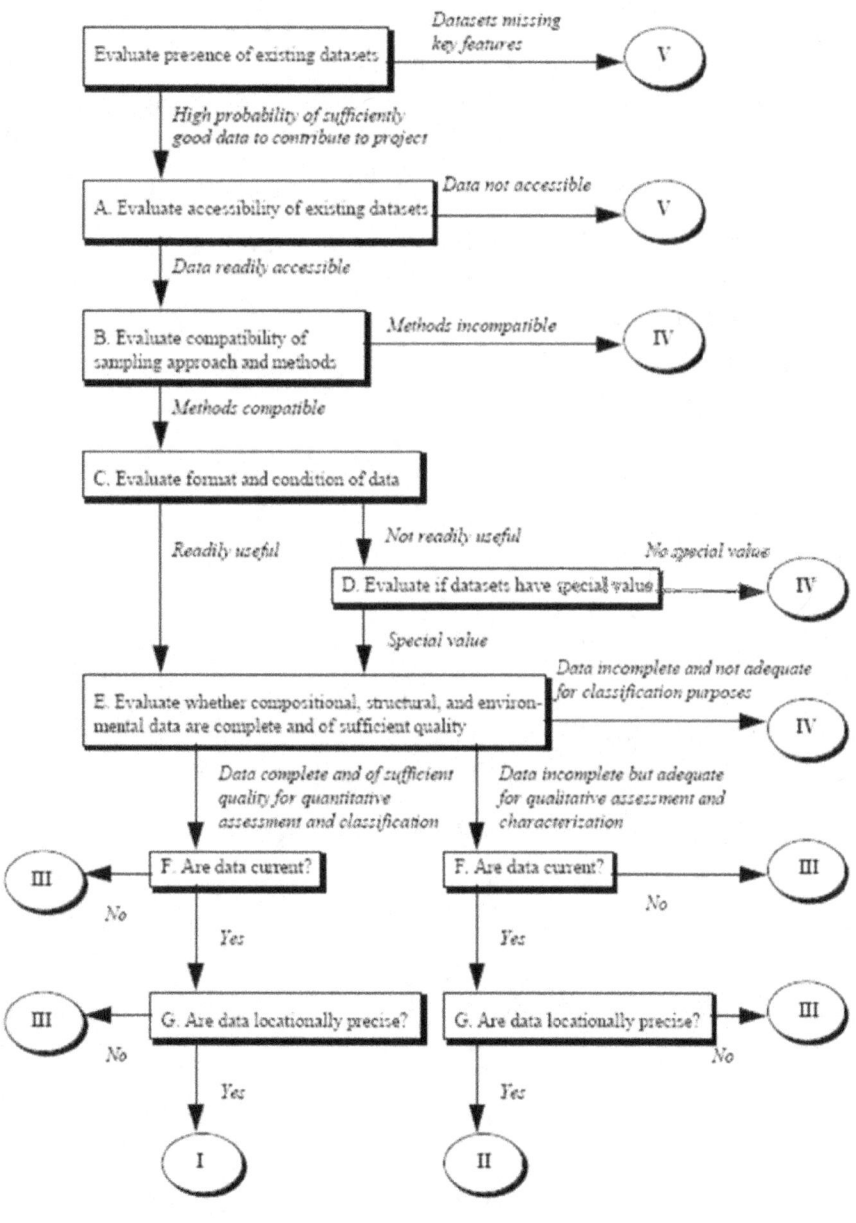

Categories of Utility for Existing Data Sets

Category Description

I.   Samples are adequate for classification and mapping (i.e., the data are geo-referenced, represent existing vegetation, and contain sufficient structural, compositional and site information to place the sample within the standard classification framework).

II.   Data are adequate to assist in photo interpretation, photographic signature key development, or map accuracy assessment (i.e., the vegetation and site information are of lower quality, but the samples represent existing vegetation and are geo-referenced with reasonable confidence).

III.   Data can be used for vegetation classification and characterization of a vegetation type within the park, but not for mapping or analysis because the sample is not adequately geo-referenced, contains inadequate detail in the vegetation information, and/or may not represent existing vegetation at the sample location.

IV.   Data set was assessed and not found to be useful at any level.

V.   Data set was not available for assessment.

Appendix 2: Support Datasets Providing Vegetation Classification Information within Amistad National Recreation Area

Table 2-1. Soils Map Units and Representative Plant Species in Amistad National Recreation Area (Source: Golden, Gabriel, and Stevens [USDA-SCS] 1982)

AMIS Soil Map Units	Diagnostic Plant Species / Comments
Acuna silty clay, 0-3% slopes (AcB)	Perennial threeawns, curly mesquite, slim tridens, tobosa, mesquite, whitebrush, paloverde, condalia, pricklypear, tasajillo / Prime Farmland
Amistad flaggy clay loam, 1-8% slopes (AmD)	Fall witchgrass, slim tridens, perennial threeawn, hairy grama, catclaw and blackbrush acacia
Amistad very flaggy loam, 8-15% slopes (ASE)	Fall witchgrass, slim tridens, perennial threeawns, hairy grama, catclaw and blackbrush acacia
Amistad Association, Rolling (ATE)	Fall witchgrass, slim tridens, perennial threeawns, hairy grama, catclaw and blackbrush acacia
Coahuila clay loam, 0-3% slopes (CoB)	Perennial threeawns, curly mesquite, slim tridens, tobosa, mesquite, whitebrush, paloverde, condalia, pricklypear, tasajillo / Prime Farmland
Dev soils, frequently flooded (De)	Buffalograss, perennial threeawns
Ector – Rock outcrop association, hilly (ERF)	Fall witchgrass, perennial threeawns, hairy grama, juniper, coyotillo, mescal bean, leatherstem
Ector – Rock outcrop association, very steep (ERG)	Hairy grama, fall witchgrass, perennial threeawns, juniper, condalia, Texas persimmon, coyotillo, ocotillo, cacti, sotol, lechuguilla, mescal bean
Felipe and Zorra soils, very rocky, 8-40% slopes (FzG)	Slim tridens, perennial threeawns, fall witchgrass, Hall panicum, blackbrush, cenizo, condalia, acacia, cacti
Hodgins silt loam, 0-3% slopes (HdB)	Tarbush, mesquite, sticky selloa, creosote bush, perennial threeawns, tobosa, burrograss / Prime Farmland
Hodgins silty clay loam, frequently flooded (Ho)	Buffalograss, perennial threeawns
Jimenez – Quemado complex, 1-8% slopes (JmD)	Perennial threeawns, slim tridens, hooded windmillgrass, fall witchgrass, cenizo, blackbrush acacia, guajillo
Lagloria loam, 0-3% slopes (LaB)	Buffalograss, curly mesquite, Bermuda grass, mesquite, huisache / Prime Farmland
Langtry cobbly silt loam, very rocky, 1-8% slopes (LnD)	Fall witchgrass, perennial threeawns, hairy grama, coyotillo, mescal bean, leatherstem
Langtry cobbly silt loam, very rocky, 8-15% slopes (LnE)	Fall witchgrass, perennial threeawns, hairy grama, coyotillo, mescal bean, leatherstem
Langtry – Rock outcrop association, rolling (LRE)	Fall witchgrass, perennial threeawns, hairy grama, coyotillo, mescal bean, leatherstem
Langtry – Rock outcrop association, very steep (LRG)	Hairy grama, fall witchgrass, perennial threeawns, condalia, Texas persimmon, leatherstem, blackbrush, lechuguilla, coyotillo, ocotillo, cacti, sotol, mescal bean
Lozier-Shumla association, undulating (LZD)	Perennial threeawns, fluffgrass, red grama, creosote bush
Mariscal very channery silt loam, 1-8% slopes (MaD)	Fall witchgrass, perennial threeawns, slim and hairy tridens, creosote bush, lechuguilla, cenizo, catclaw acacia, yucca
Mariscal – Lozier association, very steep (MLG)	Lechuguilla, hairy tridens, perennial threeawns, burrograss, slim tridens, red grama, Hall panicum, creosote bush, cenizo
Olmos very gravelly loam, 1-8% slopes (OmD)	Perennial threeawns, slim tridens, fall witchgrass, buffalograss, curly mesquite, cenizo, blackbrush
Pintas clay, frequently flooded (Pn)	Lindheimer muhly, bushy bluestem, buffalograss, curly mesquite, bermuda grass, baccharis, whitebrush
Pits (Pt)	The large borrow area below AMIS Dam is ~140 acres.

Table 2-1. Soils Map Units and Representative Plant Species in Amistad National Recreation Area (Source: Golden, Gabriel, and Stevens [USDA-SCS] 1982)

AMIS Soil Map Units	Diagnostic Plant Species / Comments
Reynosa silty clay loam (Ra)	Buffalograss, curly mesquite, Bermuda grass, mesquite, huisache / Prime Farmland
Rio Diablo silty clay (Rd)	Buffalograss, curly mesquite, perennial threeawns, tobosa, slim tridens, fall Witchgrass, mesquite, juniper, agrito, cacti, condalia / Prime Farmland
Rio Grande silt loam (Rg)	Bermuda grass, baccharis, giant reed / Prime Farmland
Rio Grande soils, frequently flooded (Ro)	Bermuda grass, baccharis
Riverwash (Rv)	Nearly barren sediment.
Sanderson – Shumla complex, 0-5% slopes (SsC)	Perennial threeawns, slim tridens, fall witchgrass, creosote bush, tarbush, tasajillo, dog cholla, pricklypear, acacia
Shumla loam, 0-5% slopes (SuC)	Perennial threeawns, slim tridens, fall witchgrass, creosote bush, tarbush, tasajillo, dog cholla, pricklypear, acacia
Tarrant association, undulating (TAD)	Fall witchgrass, perennial threeawns, hairy grama, mescal bean, leatherstem
Tobosa clay, 0-1% slopes (ToA)	Curly mesquite, perennial threeawns, tobosa, mesquite, whitebrush, spiny hackberry, condalia, cacti / Prime Farmland
Valverde silty clay loam, 0%-3% slopes (VaB)	Cenizo, mesquite, blackbrush, sticky selloa, catclaw acacia, slim tridens, perennial threeawns, buffalograss / Prime Farmland
Zapata – Vinegarron complex, 1%-5% slopes (ZaC)	Cenizo, perennial threeawns, red and hairy grama
Zorra – Rock outcrop complex, 1%-8% slopes (ZoD)	Fall witchgrass, perennial threeawns, hairy grama, blackbrush, cenizo, coyotillo, mescal bean, leatherstem
Zorra – Rock outcrop complex, 8%-15% slopes (ZoE)	Fall witchgrass, perennial threeawns, hairy grama, blackbrush, cenizo, coyotillo, mescal bean, leatherstem
Zorra – Rock outcrop association, rolling (ZRE)	Fall witchgrass, perennial threeawns, hairy grama, blackbrush, cenizo, coyotillo, mescal bean, leatherstem

NPS 621/106602, February 2011